30 Minutes
... Before a Meeting

Alan Barker

KOGAN
PAGE

YOURS TO HAVE AND TO HOLD
BUT NOT TO COPY

First published in 1997
Reprinted 1998

Kogan Page Limited
120 Pentonville Road
London
N1 9JN

© Alan Barker, 1997

British Library Cataloguing in Publication Data
A CIP record for this book is available from the British Library.

ISBN 0 7494 2356 0

Typeset by Florencetype Ltd, Stoodleigh, Devon
Printed in England by Clays Ltd, St Ives plc

CONTENTS

The 30 Minutes Series

The Kogan Page 30 Minutes Series has been devised to give your confidence a boost when faced with tackling a new skill or challenge for the first time.

So the next time you're thrown in at the deep end and want to bring your skills up to scratch or pep up your career prospects, turn to the *30 Minutes Series* for help!

Titles available are:

30 Minutes Before Your Job Interview

30 Minutes Before a Meeting

30 Minutes Before a Presentation

30 Minutes to Boost Your Communication Skills

30 Minutes to Succeed in Business Writing

30 Minutes to Master the Internet

30 Minutes to Make the Right Decision

30 Minutes to Prepare a Job Application

30 Minutes to Write a Business Plan

30 Minutes to Write a Marketing Plan

30 Minutes to Write a Report

30 Minutes to Write Sales Letters

Available from all good booksellers.
For further information on the series, please contact:

Kogan Page, 120 Pentonville Road, London N1 9JN
Tel: 0171 278 0433 Fax: 0171 837 6348

INTRODUCTION

You are about to chair a meeting. Everybody is arriving in 30 minutes. How do you feel?

Chairing is one of the most high-profile and challenging tasks for any manager. An effective meeting makes a major contribution to an organisation's success; a poor meeting can do more damage than not meeting at all.

Think back to the last meeting you attended. Was it a success? If so, why? Perhaps everybody felt that they were listened to; that their ideas were respected; that they genuinely shared responsibility for decisions. You left the room energised and committed. Everybody looked forward to the next time.

Or was it a failure? Perhaps people argued over trivia or went off at tangents. Maybe some dominated and others faded into the background, or withdrew to lick their wounds. At times the meeting may have gone out of control; or it may have been tyrannised by one person. Most importantly, it probably went on too long. You left exhausted, angry – and late for the next meeting.

The Chair usually takes the blame when things go wrong, but rarely gets credit when all goes well. The reason is that a meeting is a group in action: when people succeed as a team, they feel they have done it themselves. Your task, then, is to create the conditions in which people can give their best.

Ninety per cent of a successful meeting happens before it starts. You are already at an advantage: you have half an hour to prepare. This book will show you how.

Good luck!

1

WHY IS THE MEETING HAPPENING?
(30 minutes to go)

Key Questions

■ Why are you holding the meeting?

■ Are your objectives clear?

■ How can you help the meeting to be a success?

Your meeting is one of millions being held today around the world. Meetings are one of the commonest ways in which people communicate at work. The higher we climb the managerial ladder, the more meetings we attend. And radical changes in the way we work – project and cross-functional teams, new kinds of client partnerships – are creating ever more opportunities for meetings. Research suggests that the number of meetings at work will rise by five per cent per year for the foreseeable future.

Costing your meeting

Take a moment, right now, to estimate the cost of this meeting. Include:

- Salaries
- Administration costs (before and after the meeting)
- Travel expenses
- Equipment costs or hiring charges
- Venue charges
- Stationery, printing, postage
- Telephone charges (before or, in a teleconference, during the meeting)
- Refreshments
- Lost opportunity costs (for example, while sales staff are not selling).

What figure have you come up with? It's unlikely to be less than a few hundred pounds per hour. Ask yourself: will the outcome of the meeting justify the cost?

Survey after survey suggests that most managers consider a substantial proportion of the time they spend in meetings wasted. So why are *you* holding this meeting? What are your goals?

Is your meeting necessary?

Most meetings are held with one of four objectives in mind:

- To 'discuss'
- To decide

- To decree
- To demolish.

Ask most people why they are holding a meeting, and the immediate answer is probably: 'To discuss the issues.' But *why* are we discussing them?

'We discuss in order to make decisions', we might reply. Indeed, managers often complain that meetings fail precisely because they don't result in clear decisions. But a decision is a commitment to action, and gaining genuine commitment from a group of people can be difficult. 'Consensus' – the usual word for collective decisions – is often code for 'compromise'. Collective decisions are vulnerable to: analysis paralysis – spending an excessive time pondering unnecessary detail; the dead hand of the past – 'We've always done it this way'; or groupthink – the urge to agree at the cost of considering alternatives.

Does the whole group *have* to make the decision? Who has real responsibility for taking action? Isn't the decision theirs?

Decisions are best made by individuals. Action responsibilities and accountability are likelier to be clear. You might discuss an issue in a meeting to help you make a better decision. But Chairs sometimes hide behind the principle of collective decision making, wasting people's time on a matter that should be their sole responsibility.

Meetings are often called to present information: either by senior management, who use a 'briefing' to announce their latest decrees; or by lesser managers being 'put through their paces' in the familiar ritual of making a presentation. Meetings are probably the least effective way possible to deliver information. Most of it will be forgotten unless it's supported in writing. And if it's on paper, there is no need to reproduce it at length in a meeting.

There is one other popular reason for holding meetings: to play politics. The essence of manipulation is that it is covert. Its secret weapon is the 'hidden agenda' and its favoured strategy is to create alliances and conflicts, sow the seeds of confusion, create diversions and outmanoeuvre the competition.

Meetings 'infected' with manipulative behaviour tend to repeat themselves: the losers in one round will fight back in the next. The waste of resources in such guerrilla warfare is appalling.

Clarifying your objectives

However, there are a number of powerful reasons for calling a meeting. Use them to help you clarify your specific goals.

To exchange and evaluate information

We meet to see what others in the team are doing; to avoid duplication of tasks; to put what we are doing in context; and to see the bigger picture.

Groups can evaluate information more effectively than a single person, because they can look at it from different points of view. This results in fewer gross errors of understanding. Gathering, exchanging and evaluating information are important activities prior to making a decision. A consultation meeting – as part of staff surveys, or between a consultant and client – is a typical example.

A briefing meeting exchanges and evaluates information in a particular way. Team leaders communicate decisions and changes 'down the line'; in exchange, the team can evaluate how the changes affect their work, build their commitment to them and send their responses – and their own ideas – back 'up the line'.

To solve problems

Success in solving a problem depends on deciding what *kind* of problem it is. A problem tends to be either an obstacle or a challenge: a gap between what is and what *should* be, or between what is and what *could* be.

If you are about to tackle a problem in your meeting, ask: 'Is it an obstacle or a challenge? Something in the way, preventing us from achieving some other objective? Or an opportunity to do something new or better?'

Groups are particularly effective at handling 'fuzzy' problems. Ask yourself:

■ 'Are the *initial conditions* clear? Do we know precisely what the problem is?'

■ 'Is our *goal* clear? Do we know precisely what the solution should be? Would we be able to recognise clearly when we have solved the problem?'

■ 'Is the *gap* between initial conditions and our goal strictly measurable?'

■ 'Are the *operators* clear? Can we exactly describe the means of getting from initial conditions to our goal, in terms of procedures, resources, personnel? Is the process of solving the problem clear?'

If any of your answers to these questions is 'No', the problem is probably suitable for group treatment. Groups can:

■ Create a more detailed description of the problem itself

■ Widen the terms of reference

■ Find new perspectives

■ Explore alternative solutions

■ Place the problem – and possible solutions – in a wider context.

11

Groups are not good at solving well-structured or 'one-right-answer' problems, where the initial conditions, the goal and the operators are all clear. So problems needing expert knowledge or complex reasoning are best handled by individuals; a group will only think as well as its most competent member.

To resolve conflict

The obvious example is a negotiation, which aims to find the source of the conflict, alternative approaches to the situation and new ways for resolving it.

But conflict can arise in any meeting. Problem solving and evaluating information can themselves cause arguments which the meeting must resolve if it is to progress. And building or repairing people's morale at a time of change and uncertainty can often mean resolving conflicts.

To inspire

Humans are biologically gregarious. Very few of us can get through a day comfortably without interacting with others. We *like* to meet, especially if our work tends to isolate us. Meetings help us to find meaning in our work by relating it to the work of others; they can support us through difficulties by allowing us to share problems; they can energise and motivate us.

So, establish the purpose of your meeting. Your statement of purpose should revolve around a verb. What are you going to *do* – apart from talk?

If you are going to address a number of tasks, they should be connected in some way. Are they all *relevant* to all the members of the group? Is the meeting *necessary* to carry them all out? Some tasks might be dealt with more efficiently in 'mini-meetings' before or after the main meeting.

What do you want to *achieve*? Consider: the ideal outcome; the realistic outcome; a fallback position.

What *decisions* will be taken in the meeting? Who will take them? Why must they be taken *at the meeting*? Are *resources* available to carry out any actions you anticipate? Is *anybody else* going to be affected? Should they be consulted – or invited to the meeting?

If you have an agenda, repeat this process for each agenda item.

Focus on *outcomes*. What results are you looking for? How will you know that you've achieved them?

Are these objectives clearly stated on the agenda? If not, you will have to make them clear to the group at the start of the meeting: using a flipchart or whiteboard will help focus the group's thinking on your goal.

Why meetings fail

Look at your objectives. Review them against this check-list of questions:

■ Is the meeting necessary to achieve them?

■ Are the objectives of the meeting clear?

■ Are you clear what problems need to be tackled?

■ Are they obstacles or challenges? Well structured or fuzzy?

■ Do you have the means to keep the group's thinking focused: agenda, clock, flipchart or board?

■ Is it the right time to be holding the meeting?

There are numerous reasons why meetings fail:

The meeting is unnecessary

The job could be done more simply or cheaply. Maybe it is routine and doesn't need to be discussed, or you can exchange information on paper or electronically. Perhaps only one or two people need to be involved, or the problem needs the attention of a single expert. Or perhaps there is nothing to be done at all!

The meeting is held for the wrong reason

To discuss, to decree or to demolish: all common reasons for holding meetings, and all inadequate. Managers often call meetings merely to wield power over others, or to pursue some private agenda. They use the meeting to rubber-stamp decisions – or as a steamroller. Many meetings happen as a matter of habit: a habit which nobody dares challenge. Or they are primarily social occasions: a chance to 'get away from the desk'. Meetings of this kind are group therapy in disguise: they are held to avoid loneliness.

The objective of the meeting is unclear

Nobody has asked why the meeting is being held. Nobody knows its purpose; they have not received or read any of the supporting papers. The agenda is vague and unhelpful, or doesn't exist.

The wrong people are there

Nobody present has the authority to make the required decisions. Or the right people are absent: substitutes are sent at the last minute, who are poorly briefed and unable to take responsibility.

Lack of proper control

The procedure of the meeting is unclear; timekeeping is appalling; the discussion rambles from point to point; hidden agendas hijack the proceedings; conflict, when it occurs, is not properly managed. Blame for any or all of these problems is usually laid at the feet of a weak Chair;

but a dictatorial Chair, who represses discussion rather than controlling it, can be just as damaging.

Poor environment

The venue is inappropriate or uncomfortable; facilities are poor; disruptions destroy concentration.

Poor timing

It's the wrong time of day/week/month/year; the meeting fails to start or end on time; people arrive late or leave early.

Your meeting won't improve by magic. You must *want* change and be willing to do something to achieve it; and you may need to convince others in the meeting that they want it too.

The golden rules of effective meetings

As you work on your objectives, remember these three golden rules.

1. Every meeting is unique

A meeting is too expensive to hold for no good reason. If you can't find one, or if your objectives can be achieved in other ways, ask yourself whether the meeting is necessary. This is particularly true if it is a regular meeting: a weekly team meeting, a project meeting or committee meeting. The agenda *must* be unique.

2. A meeting's success is judged by the actions that result from it

If our only agreement at the end of the meeting is to hold another meeting, something has gone seriously wrong. Promise to write an action list after the meeting. On the list, you should allocate responsibility for each action to a named individual, with a specific deadline. Who will monitor progress? Promise yourself, also, to review the action list after the meeting, asking whether you could have agreed any of those actions *without* holding the meeting. This will help you make the next one more efficient!

3. Running a meeting is the responsibility of the whole group

Primary responsibility for the meeting's success must rest with the Chair (or the person who called the meeting). But every participant should contribute to making the meeting work. The minute-taker can help the Chair to keep time, to check actions agreed and to record the meeting's progress and outcomes. As Chair, you can become a coach, guiding the meeting, developing people's skills and leading by example.

2

WHO IS ATTENDING?
(25 minutes to go)

Key questions

- Are the right people attending?
- Can you make particular people responsible for agenda items?
- Does anybody have a special role to play?
- Can you help to balance the group's task objectives with its social objectives?
- Have you briefed the administrator/minute-taker adequately?

As Chair, your job will be to ensure that people participate fully and contribute positively. What can you do before the meeting to help facilitate this?

Taking the chair

Who's in charge? You are! But is there a good reason for you to take command? Or is it merely force of habit? You could rotate the role of Chair so that everybody in the team has the opportunity to experience that responsibility. At the very least, people may be less likely to 'misbehave' when they know that it will be their turn to keep order next time!

Taking the Chair means: not taking the minutes; and not acting as a participant. Your job will be to manage the meeting, which is difficult enough. If you have to make a contribution, give a presentation or take minutes, you will make chairing virtually impossible to do well.

Who is participating?

Are they the right people? What is their *relevance* to the meeting's purpose? Are there any particular kinds of contribution you want them to make, or that they intend to make? Perhaps they are:

- Key decision makers
- Experts or givers of information
- People who need information
- Opinion formers
- Senior managers with an interest in the decisions to be reached
- Arbitrators in potential disputes
- Friends, consultants or guests.

Are they *able to attend*? The more valuable they are to the meeting, the less likely they are to be available! Will a deputy or last minute substitute be acceptable? What do they *need* to prepare for the meeting? Should you brief them or send them papers: the minutes of the last meeting; reports; the latest figures?

Look over your agenda and try to allocate names to items. Who is responsible for the task under discussion? Who will need to take the critical decision? Who will carry it through? Consider putting them in charge of the task, allowing you to oversee the conversation.

What roles do you expect people to play? A role is a set of behaviours by which we can help the meeting achieve its objectives. Most of us tend to contribute to groups in consistent ways. We can broadly categorise these types as:

- Ideas people
- Action people
- Administrators
- Carers.

Ideally, the group should contain a balance of all four. To adjust the balance in the group, you may need to ask some-body to play a certain role more strongly than normal.

Roles in meetings

Ideas people

Typical behaviours

- Advancing new ideas and strategies
- Focusing on major issues
- Tackling problem solving creatively
- Exploring and reporting on ideas and developments beyond the meeting
- Making contacts outside the group

Positive qualities

- Imagination, intellect, knowledge

- Willing to explore
- Can make contact with others

Possible weaknesses

- May disregard practical details, rules or regulations
- Short attention span

Action people

Typical behaviours

- Influencing the way the meeting's thinking is channelled
- Focusing on objectives and priorities
- Pushing towards a decision
- Turning concepts and plans into practical working procedures
- Maintaining a sense of urgency

Positive qualities

- Drive and a readiness to challenge inertia, ineffectiveness, complacency and self-deception
- Capacity to follow through
- Self-discipline

Possible weaknesses

- Prone to provocation, irritation and impatience
- Lack of flexibility
- May be unresponsive to new or unproven ideas

Administrators

Typical behaviours

- Analysing problems, evaluating ideas and suggestions for practicability
- Ensuring nothing has been overlooked

- Checking details
- Carrying out agreed plans systematically and efficiently

Positive qualities

- Organisational ability, practicality, common sense
- Judgement, discretion, hard-headedness

Possible weaknesses

- May lack inspiration and the ability to motivate others
- Tendency to worry about details
- Reluctant to let go

Carers

Typical behaviours

- Coordinating the meeting's progress towards objectives
- Making best use of the group's resources
- Maximising the potential of each team member
- Building on suggestions
- Improving communication between group members

Positive qualities

- Welcomes all contributions on their merit
- Strong sense of objectives
- Ability to respond to people and situations
- Promotes team spirit

Possible weaknesses

- May try to avoid conflict
- May be indecisive in moments of crisis

Many meetings fail because the group is dominated by one or two roles. This situation often arises in teams made up of professional or technical specialists promoted to managerial positions. A group of *ideas people* may be enormously creative but never get anything done. A group of *action people* may spend all their time arguing about what to do, pitching one solution against another without investigating causes or different perspectives on the problem. A group of *administrators* may pay great attention to 'the dots and commas' but fail to come up with new solutions. A group of *carers* may look after each other but fail to address difficult or contentious issues.

How groups work

The group may be meeting only once. It may be a newly formed team or a regular committee. Your task will be to manage them *as a group*. Thinking about how groups work will allow you to:

■ Understand better what's going on in the meeting

■ Appreciate how conversation in the meeting differs from other kinds of conversation

■ Improve the output or results of the meeting.

We can define a group as any number of people who interact in some way, are aware of each other and perceive themselves to be a group. A group, by this definition, is limited in number to about 12. Any larger meeting will have difficulty evolving as a single group – and sub-groups will probably emerge. The ideal number for an internal business meeting is between six and nine.

Any group is made up of individuals. Once introduced into a group, we pursue four essential aims:

■ A sense of well-being (physical, mental, emotional, economic, spiritual)

■ A sense of belonging

- Recognition from the group
- Control over our own lives.

If the group satisfies these needs, we respond by strengthening it. If we feel 'left out', we withdraw – physically or mentally – or pursue some other strategy. Watch out for the signs of withdrawal:

- Refusing to speak
- Sitting back from the table
- Looking down at the table or floor
- Insistent doodling or fiddling
- Provocative or hostile comments
- Defensive responses to other people's remarks
- Seeking support within the group.

Look at the list of attendees. Imagine them together. Do they form a natural group? How well do they know each other? What are their interests, aims, ambitions, or assumptions about each other? Are all of these reconcilable within the group?

The group may be *formal* or *informal*. Formal groups are consciously created – usually from outside the group – to accomplish particular tasks or fulfil specific functions. Teams are formal groups. Informal groups, by contrast, grow spontaneously. Informal groups, broadly speaking, satisfy the human needs that formal groups neglect or ignore. Your meeting will probably contain elements of both kinds of group.

Put simply, extremely formal groups tend to work too hard to enjoy themselves while extremely informal groups tend to spend too much time having fun to do any work.

The most formal of groups need rigorous procedures to prevent them splintering. The rules of AGMs and other large meetings are designed to allow everybody to contribute, prevent hijacking, and ensure that the meeting's business is completed on time. If you are about to chair a meeting involving more than a dozen people, concentrate on the formal protocols that will help you to keep order.

Points of order: Formal meetings

- Make sure that you are aware of the rules governing your meeting. They may be written down in a constitution or other company document

- Have you given adequate notice of the meeting? You may be required to give a certain minimum number of days' (or working days') notice

- Can you operate only with a quorum? You may not be able to pass resolutions or even carry on the meeting's business without it

- Do you operate a system of motions, proposals and amendments? A motion is normally put to the meeting prior to discussion and may be circulated with the agenda. After discussion, a proposal is submitted to the meeting; proposers and seconders identify themselves for the original motion, and for any amendments that have arisen during the discussion

- What rules of debate do you operate? In the most formal of meetings, all remarks are addressed through the Chair

- Do minutes have to be taken in a particular way?

A group's first priority is to survive. In pursuit of that goal, they have two kinds of objective: task objectives and social objectives.

Task objectives concern the job to be done and may be imposed or dictated from outside the group. Social objectives relate to the group's developing sense of identity and well-being. They usually develop from within the group. The group in your meeting will pursue both task and social objectives. One of your most important tasks as Chair is to *balance* them so that the group coheres and becomes more productive. Problems may arise if:

- Task objectives are obscured by social objectives (the group is having too much of a good time)
- Task objectives suppress or damage social objectives (tasks imposed dictatorially, for example, or when the group is under stress)
- The two kinds of objective come into conflict (for example, one part of the group seeking to impose tasks on another).

So how can you achieve this delicate balance? Here are some specific actions you might consider taking. You may not feel able to manage all of them at this meeting. Pick a few and concentrate on achieving them:

- Make task objectives clear
- Thank people for their contributions
- Encourage different points of view by distinguishing clearly between ideas and the people expressing them
- Challenge judgemental statements for relevance and ask for evidence
- Encourage people to cooperate
- Challenge behaviour that threatens or subverts the group: political remarks, evidence of hidden agendas, personal attacks
- Give people responsibility. Trust people to be honest, and to fulfil their promises

- Remind the group of the objective of the conversation. Move things forward rather than harping on the past
- Emphasise group achievements
- Limit chat and gossip.

Liaising with the meeting's administrator

The administrator of the meeting is usually more than a minute-taker – important though that function is. They will often be responsible for much of the preparation for the meeting, arrangements during the meeting and follow-up after it.

Common complaints voiced by meeting administrators are that they:

- Have been brought in at a moment's notice
- Are unclear what their responsibilities are
- Haven't been told what style to adopt in writing minutes
- Don't understand what people are talking about
- Don't know the participants or their names
- Cannot follow a conversation because it is disorderly
- Get bored during the meeting through lack of involvement
- Are unclear what has been agreed or resolved
- Have their minutes 'doctored' or 'censored' by the Chair (or others).

You can forestall many of these problems. Involve the administrator in your preparations. Make sure that you have agreed:

- The purpose of the meeting
- Who is attending

- What will go on the agenda
- Background information to help in taking the minutes.

How will you record the meeting's progress? The administrator will be able to take the minutes more effectively if they have the authority to:

- Intervene to clarify points that are unclear
- Summarise at the end of each item with details of decisions and actions agreed.

Talk together about these matters *before the meeting*. The administrator can be invaluable in helping the Chair to keep time, keep to the agenda and keep order. Taking on these responsibilities will make administering the meeting more satisfying.

3

WHAT'S ON THE AGENDA?
(20 minutes to go)

Key questions

- Do you have an agenda?
- Is it written down?
- Does it give instructions to the meeting – or is it only a list of headings?
- Does your agenda include 'Any other business'? Do you need it?
- Is the meeting's timetable clear, both overall and for each item?
- Do you plan to take refreshments while meeting? Is this necessary?

Whoever controls the agenda controls the meeting. If the agenda is not made public, the meeting may be hijacked: the result will be confusion, frustration and failure.

A written agenda allows everyone to focus on what they are to do before, during and after the meeting. It acts as a plan of the meeting to help people prepare, an objective control of the meeting's progress, and a measure of the meeting's success. You are responsible for setting the agenda. After all, *you're* calling the meeting. If you already have a written agenda, can you improve it in any way? If you don't, it's not too late to write one! A single piece of paper including the matters you wish to deal with, or a list on flipchart, is better than nothing. Involve your administrator if you can.

Making full use of the agenda

The word 'agenda' is Latin for 'things to be done', so each agenda item is a task. Its entry on the agenda should indicate:

- What the task is
- How it will be tackled
- What the group will do at the end of the item
- A condition of satisfaction: how we will know we've achieved what we set out to do.

Every item on the agenda, therefore, should contain at least one *verb*, indicating what the group will *do*.

For example, '*Item 3: New IT network*' says very little that will help participants to prepare. Compare: '*Item 3: New IT network*'. *Clive* <u>to present</u> *quotations and essential specifications of systems under consideration. Team* <u>to agree</u> *system to be recommended for purchase.* This much fuller entry indicates what the group is to do, who has a key responsibility in carrying out the task, and how we will know whether we have achieved our objective.

Contents of an agenda: Checklist

The most formal of agendas will include (in this order):

- Title of meeting
- Date, time, venue
- Apologies for absence
- Minutes of previous meeting
- Matters arising from the previous meeting
- Other items to be discussed and decided
- Motions relating to the above
- Reports from sub-committees
- Contributions from guest speakers
- Any other business
- Date, time and venue of next meeting

Your agenda may not need to be so comprehensive. Consider the advantages of including timings for each item and 'owners' for each item.

Constructing the agenda

As you gather items for the agenda, look for:

- A logical order
- A common thread: keep linked items together
- Routine items: place near the beginning
- Special factors (for example, people who are only involved in a part of the meeting)
- Difficult or contentious items.

In particular, distinguish between urgent items and important ones. Place urgent matters needing little work at the start of the meeting. Important matters needing closer and longer attention are best positioned towards the middle when the group's physical and mental alertness are at their peak. Put the 'easiest' items – those of greatest interest, perhaps, or presentations by guest speakers – towards the end.

The shape of the agenda should also reflect the thinking process that you wish to follow. Clarify for yourself the objective of each item, perhaps by casting it as a 'How to', and then ask how the meeting might best think its way towards the goal.

There is more about managing the thinking process of a meeting in Chapter 5. For the moment, it is useful to remember that every group thinking task will probably move through four broad stages:

- **Evidence**: what we know about the matter

- **Interpretation**: what we think about the evidence, different perspectives and implications

- **Opportunities**: possible plans of action based on our interpretation, what actions are available to us, how we might achieve the objective

- **Action**: which opportunities we choose to pursue.

Be careful to emphasise these stages in your agenda. Many meetings jump over crucial stages in the thinking process, in the rush to achieve results. Making the steps clear on the agenda itself will help you to manage the group's thinking more effectively.

Assembling the agenda

- Remove any unnecessary items
- Give detailed titles to each item
- Every title should contain at least one verb: what the group will *do*
- Give timings to each item
- Indicate any specific speakers to an item
- Note any attached papers – in case of loss
- Consider putting motions on a separate sheet, for ease of reference.

Beware 'Any other business'! If something is worth discussing, it should be itemised on the agenda. All too often, people use 'AOB' to pursue private or hidden agendas, to settle old scores, reawaken old grudges or make lengthy and irrelevant complaints. If you can, remove this item from the agenda. Remember that your meeting should end on a positive note, with a summary of what you have achieved and the suggested next steps.

How to avoid 'any other business'

- Distribute a draft agenda, with invitations for contributions
- Invite participants to submit any late business at the start of the meeting
- Decide whether to include extra items, on the basis of their urgency, not their importance. Make it clear that any late inclusions are at the Chair's discretion
- Amend the agenda. Consider placing the new items at the beginning of the meeting, rather than at the end

■ Allocate time to the new items and revise the timings for the rest of the agenda. Keep to the original overall timing of the meeting; simply extending it is counter-productive.

Watching the clock

Some Chairs seem to make it a point of honour to have meetings that last for hours. But a successful meeting depends on how well everybody participates, not on how long it is.

Set a time to finish. Announce it on the agenda – and stick to it! No meeting, or part of a meeting, should last longer than 90 minutes. If the meeting must last longer, build in break times, with suitable refreshments.

Fit the items on the agenda to the available time. Timings for individual items are useful here: if you find you can allocate only a few minutes to an important item, you are over-filling the agenda. Consider other ways to save time. It may be possible, for example, to arrange the meeting in conjunction with others.

Making your meeting shorter

■ Announce a finishing time. It's discourteous not to

■ Limit the number of items on the agenda to the time allowed

■ Allocate a task owner to each item, who will take responsibility for any decision. You can even cross-reference the time taken on each item against the owners to show who uses time most – or least – efficiently!

■ Impose a time limit on each agenda item

- Allow time for breaks
- Prepare procedures for unresolved business
- Make it your goal to end on time!

The timing of the meeting can greatly affect its success.

Many meetings arrange their own times. It must be today, the conference room is only available at 2pm, and so on. Within the inevitable constraints of a busy organisation, do what you can to influence these matters for the best. Research suggests that the best time for thinking is late morning. Meeting at the end of the day might make meetings shorter; but it might not make them better.

Try to separate meeting from eating, and hold the meeting first. Lunch is a powerful incentive to end on time, and people will be more alert before eating than after. If you cannot avoid including food in the meeting, take a few precautions.

- Decide on your own private agenda. Are you going to meet – or eat?
- If the meeting is worth attending, you must be prepared not to eat much
- Avoid alcohol
- Taking notes will be difficult. Arm yourself with a narrow pad which can slip easily between plates and glasses.

4

WHERE ARE YOU MEETING?
(15 minutes to go)

Key questions

- Is the meeting room appropriate to your purpose?
- Can you adapt the room to meet your needs?
- Can you alter the layout of the furniture?
- Do you have all the equipment you need?
- Are you adequately prepared for technology: computers, telephone, video?

The venue can have a powerful effect on the outcome of your meeting. You may be unable to do much about the venue of your meeting at this late stage, but some aspects may be adaptable.

35

Preparing the venue

Is the venue conveniently located? Is it accessible: for people with disabilities, for example, or women travelling alone at night?

Are you meeting on 'home ground'? Will everybody feel at ease when they are there – or will they be intimidated by the trophies of a dominant senior manager? If the meeting is in a hotel or conference venue, you will need to liaise to establish timings, numbers and catering, as well as establishing some protocol for that perennial issue, smoking.

Is the room the right size and shape? If we feel crowded, we will interact less and feel more stressed. On the other hand, small groups cohere more quickly in a small space. If you are holding a team meeting in a large room, create your own space by blocking off the rest of the room with screens.

Is the room suitable for your purpose? Consider:

- Acoustics
- Heating, lighting and ventilation
- Chairs: quantity and comfort
- Tables: size, flexibility and sturdiness
- Equipment and power points
- Procedures: fire drill, refreshments, toilets, telephones
- Security: thin walls, intercoms or sound systems
- Distractions: air-conditioning, trains, noise, the view, interruptions.

Are the fittings:

- Fixed: walls, windows, doors
- Semi-fixed: partitions, seating, projection screens, whiteboards
- Movable: chairs, tables, equipment?

Be careful not to mistake semi-fixed fittings for fixed! You may lose an opportunity to adapt the room to your needs.

Mind the furniture!

The style of the meeting should govern the layout of the furniture. You may wish to place allies (or potential troublemakers!) in 'control positions', while the administrator should be able to communicate easily with everybody while taking the minutes. Everybody should be able to see a screen or flipchart with a minimum of disruption. Participants should be about one arm's length from each other. Closer, and they will invade each other's space; further apart, they will feel isolated and the group dynamics will suffer. Remember, too, that effective interaction depends on easy eye contact.

Chairs should be comfortable enough to avoid numbness, but not so comfortable that people can snooze! Chairs with arms may be preferable for lengthy sessions. A table can be a barrier to good conversation, particularly if it is large or if people are not arranged equally around it. Of course, some of your group may prefer the 'protection' of a heavy table.

Planning the room layout

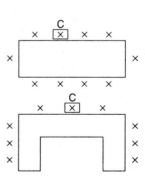

Conference

Formal

Hierarchical

Horseshoe
Easier eye contact
Promotes interaction
Strong control positions

Public horseshoe
Presents a unified group
to an audience

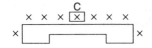

Theatre
Accommodates large
numbers
Presentational
Interaction difficult
Demands formal rules

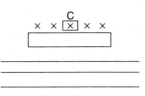

Cabaret
For work in small groups
Informal
Can be difficult to focus
attention

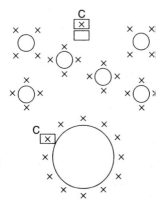

Round table
Democratic
Difficult to make presentations

Equipment and technology

If people are taking notes, or if you are providing reports
or briefing papers, supply spare copies, writing paper, pens
and pencils. If you are using a flipchart to record ideas
make sure everybody can see it clearly and delegate writing.
Sightlines are equally important when participants use an
overhead projector or computer-generated visual aids. Be
ready to darken the room for maximum effect.

Increasingly, participants attend meetings with their personal computers. Some organisations now use software that links the laptops in a meeting into a network. This is a useful tool for focusing and disciplining the meeting's thinking, but it may also present a new barrier: people may not contribute well if their eyes are glued to the screen in front of them.

Usually a meeting happens in one room or in one place, but teleconferences are increasingly common. Meetings using telephone, video or computer links can cut costs and save time but they rely on everybody being in place, on time. Lack of physical presence also puts greater pressure on the participants to use words well – and to listen carefully.

Allow pauses between speakers

A single word overlapping another speaker will cause considerable delay while the last remark is laboriously repeated. A teleconference has its own peculiar rhythm which is easily picked up with a little practice.

Use names frequently

Announce yourself by name, particularly if you haven't spoken for some time. Announce whom you are addressing, and who you would like to speak next.

Choose your words with care

The fact that people are not physically together means great weight is placed on the words used. There is a lot of scope for misunderstanding in the absence of a visual component.

Avoid hidden agendas

Teleconferences without video are vulnerable to conspiracies: notes passed silently between participants in one room, gestures and facial expressions mocking the ignorance of participants at the other end of the line. Maintain order! Of course, it can sometimes be easier to be brutally frank when the other person is 500 miles away.

On video, ensure that everybody is visible

Hidden voices and disembodied hands swimming into shot are distracting.

5

HOW WILL YOU CHAIR?
(10 minutes to go)

Key questions

- How can you make the atmosphere in the meeting as supportive as possible?
- What style of chairing do you intend to adopt?
- Can you allocate task leadership to individual group members?
- Do you have a prepared procedure for opening the meeting?
- Do you anticipate adversarial thinking?
- Can you structure the group's thinking?
- How could you improve the quality of the conversation?
- What difficult situations do you foresee?
- How will you close the meeting?

It is in meetings that our leadership skills are most publicly displayed. The effective Chair:

- Keeps the group focused on its *task*
- Finds opportunities to use the talents of every *individual*
- Develops a climate in which people can think and work as a *team*.

A group of people contains a certain amount of potential energy. People will use as much energy as necessary to survive in the group. Whatever is left, they will devote to the task. The more supportive the group climate, the less energy we need to devote to survival and the more we can give to the task. As Chair, you should do everything you can to create that supportive climate.

Establishing your style

How you do this will depend very much on the style of chairing that you choose. One of the most common criticisms of Chairs is that they are too autocratic; another is that they fail to maintain sufficient control! Many Chairs feel that they must steer the meeting towards the results that they, the Chair, require. This 'command and control' approach is almost guaranteed to fail. Not only does it cause resentment and frustration, it makes impossible demands on the Chair, who feels compelled to take responsibility for both the *content* of the meeting – the work to be done – and its *process*. We are asking the Chair to be, in effect, pilot and air traffic controller simultaneously!.

However, there may be times when you have to take a firm line: at the start of a meeting; when a group is large, newly formed, or undisciplined. 'Command and control' is undoubtedly necessary, too, in a crisis, or when the discussion involves:

- Health and safety
- Hiring and firing
- Confidentiality
- A large number of routine items.

But the best leaders use their authority to *liberate* the talents of those they lead.

Task leader or process director?

The key to effective chairing is to split the three responsibilities – for task, process and recording the meeting – and allocate them to different people.

The task leader takes responsibility for the conversation's content: defining objectives, evaluating information, solving problems, making decisions. Delegate task leadership to the group member whose job is most closely affected by the item being discussed. You, the Chair, now become process director, overseeing communication and creating the climate necessary for effective thinking. Whatever you do, delegate the job of minute-taking. *You cannot chair effectively if you are taking a record*. The minute-taker can support you by assuming other important responsibilities, such as summarising at the end of items and time-keeping.

Roles in the meeting now divide into:

- **Chair or process director**: Managing the group's social objectives, specifying the kind of thinking necessary for the task, suggesting techniques for solving problems, controlling the flow of the conversation
- **Task leader**: Specifying task objectives, focusing on results, evaluating information, measuring the success of outcomes

- **Administrator**: supporting the Chair, recording the meeting's actions and results, reflecting progress back to the meeting in regular summaries, time-keeping

- **Participants as resources**: Contributing ideas and information as suggested and authorised by the Chair to help the task leader meet the task objectives.

Opening the meeting

Make the procedural conventions clear at the opening of the meeting: participants will perform better if they know what is expected of them. Lead by example. If you abide by your own rules, people will tend to do the same.

- **Start on time**: If you don't, you'll have late arrivals next time. Start a meeting promptly and people will soon get the message

- **State the purpose or objective of the meeting**: Refer to the agenda. Indicate the common ground that exists within the group to reach this goal

- **Make all suitable introductions**: Check that everybody knows each other. Welcome new members and make apologies for absentees

- **Announce procedures and the timetable of the meeting**: Announce how long the meeting will last, and times of breaks. Indicate how you expect people to contribute, and how you intend to control the conversation.

Take each item separately, and in order. Make it clear which item the meeting is addressing, and discipline participants who stray into other items.

- Refer to the agenda

- Don't start a new item before concluding the previous one
- Clarify the item's purpose
- Identify the task leader
- Remind the group how much time is allocated.

The task leader should now specify the task objective and the reasons for discussing it, the required outcomes, and the conditions of satisfaction: how we will know that we have achieved our goals. Be ready to focus the meeting's attention again and again on these goals, outcomes and measures of success.

Adversarial thinking

Controlling the group's thinking is at the very heart of effective chairing. It's a difficult skill to acquire. Few of us have been taught many thinking techniques; we may even feel it wrong to 'tell people how to think'. Undisciplined thinking, however, is wasteful and can poison the meeting's atmosphere. A conversation without rules – and a Chair to keep them – becomes a verbal free-for-all, in which only the loudest and most persistent survive. The polite name for such quarrelling is *adversarial thinking*.

We endure endless arguments in meetings because, for many of us, adversarial thinking is the only form of organised thinking we know. It appears in four forms.

Critical thinking

The rationale behind critical thinking is presumably that, by identifying an idea's weaknesses, we can strengthen it. But we usually take criticism personally, and try to defend the idea, demolish the criticism – or attack the critic.

45

Ego thinking

When we have to defend ideas as if we were defending ourselves, ideas become opinions. Opinions are ideas gone cold. They are our assumptions about what might or should be generally true, rather than what is true in specific circumstances. They can be: stories (about what happened what may have happened, why it may have happened) explanations (for why something went wrong, or why we failed); justifications (for taking action or not); wrong-making (I am right, you are wrong); gossip (to make us feel better at the expense of others); or generalisations (to save us the trouble of thinking). We are so used to opinions that we easily mistake them for the truth. Whenever you hear the word 'fact' in a meeting, you can be almost certain that somebody is voicing an opinion.

Political thinking

When ideas become opinions, voicing an idea becomes a political act. To attack an idea is to attack its sponsor to support it is to create an alliance. We use conversation to create 'power bases' and undermine 'opponents' manipulate ideas, send up smoke screens, foment dissent or rumour.

Rigid thinking

All thinking starts from assumptions about reality Adversarial thinking merely pits these assumptions against each other. We usually call this 'debate'. Any thinking that questions the underlying assumptions is 'irrelevant'. Ideas cannot develop in a debate, because, if they are to survive attack, they must become rigid.

Rigid thinking is usually the result of: conforming to authority ('if senior management see it this way, it must be

46

right'); the influence of custom ('our profession has thought like this for the last 200 years'); habit ('this is the way we think around here'); wilful ignorance ('thinking like this saves us the bother of dealing with inconvenient detail or finding out more').

Nothing damages the thinking in meetings more than adversarial thinking, yet we accord it enormous prestige. Managers who can defend their ideas and beat off aggressive criticism become heroes; they may even be promoted on the basis of their 'strong character'. Adversarial thinking becomes a self-perpetuating cold war of argument and counter-argument.

If you want to improve the quality of the thinking in your meeting, you must help it to break out of this cycle. There are a number of tactics you can adopt.

- To counter *critical thinking*, ask specifically for positive responses to an idea: 'What's good about it?'

- To counter *ego thinking*, ask for evidence to support opinions. Ask: 'In what circumstances?' Challenge remarks for their relevance to objectives

- To counter *political thinking*, invite the whole group to think systematically. Ask for positive and negative responses to an idea in order. Develop this approach by using tools such as SWOT analysis (strengths, weaknesses, opportunities and threats), asking the group to concentrate on one aspect at a time

- To counter *rigid thinking*, ask: 'What if?' Look deliberately for the assumptions behind ideas and challenge them. Ask how the matter would look from a radically different perspective. Turn ideas upside down and see what happens.

Managing the thinking process

We can structure our thinking about an issue into four stages. Each stage requires its own conversation. Most meetings will include all four. Often they will be happening simultaneously! They will only be effective if conducted *in order*.

Evidence

In this conversation, we explore how we perceive the objective or problem, the background to the issue and the detailed information surrounding the issue. Important questions in this conversation include:

- What is our objective?
- How can we define the problem?
- Who has responsibility for the problem – who is the task leader?
- How do we see things? What are our priorities?
- In what ways do people see the evidence similarly, or differently?
- How can we understand each other?

This first conversation is often tentative, awkward, rushed or ignored. Many meetings leap towards solutions without properly investigating what the problem is! Remember that the problem may look different to different people.

Interpretation

This conversation is about how we can make sense of the evidence. The aim is to create *consensus*: an agreed vision of reality. We achieve consensus best by investigating and comparing people's perceptions. We can do this by:

- Deliberately trying to look at something from a different angle

- Asking for differing interpretations
- Distinguishing what we see from our interpretation of it
- Isolating one element of a situation and concentrating on it
- Relating elements to a bigger picture.

Manage this conversation with great care. It can easily become adversarial: most arguments are between different versions of reality. People must know that we are looking for new ways of looking. People should feel able to speculate, to utter ambiguous or half-formed ideas. Prohibit judgement and discourage criticism. Listen for the words 'right' or 'wrong'. An interpretation may be neither; it may be appropriate from one point of view but limited from another. Make it clear that no decisions will be taken in this conversation: that people are not committing themselves to action. Make it clear that you don't welcome inappropriate jokes, personal comments or emotional 'explosions'. If people do respond emotionally, acknowledge the emotion openly and distinguish it from the idea accompanying it.

Opportunities

This conversation is about assessing what we could do on the basis of our agreed interpretation. Many of the good ideas generated in meetings never become reality because no clear path of opportunity is mapped out. In this conversation, we map out such paths.

The bridge from interpretation to opportunity is *measurement* or *conditions of satisfaction*: targets, milestones, obstacles, measures of success. Don't lose sight of the original objective. We often plan by starting from where we are and planning forwards. Opportunities can become more imaginative and exciting when we place ourselves in a future where we have achieved our objective and 'plan backwards'.

Questions in this conversation should include:

- Where can we act?
- What interpretations can we build on?
- How do we judge when we have achieved our objective?
- What would we need to do to achieve this?
- Who else would be involved?
- What does the future look like?
- How can we plan our way towards it?

Action

Translating opportunity into action requires more than agreement: we must generate a promise – a commitment to action. If we take that commitment for granted, we can create resentment in others. If we make too many commitments, we can cause ourselves stress.

A conversation for action is a dynamic between requesting and promising. I ask you to do something by a certain time. I make it clear that this is a request, not an order. Orders may get immediate results; but they are unlikely to get more than the minimum, and they may not achieve results next time. You have four possible responses to this request: you may accept; you may decline; you may commit to accept or decline later ('I'll let you know by . . .'); or you may make a counter-offer ('No, but I can do something else for you . . .'). The conversation will result in a promise: 'I will do "x" for you by time "y"'.

These four conversations must be conducted *in order*. The success of each depends on the success of the conversation before it. An unresolved conversation will continue within the next one, sometimes *in code*. Unresolved aspects of a conversation for evidence may become hidden agendas. People may feel that vital evidence is being ignored to support a favoured interpretation. Interpretations unexplored may become missed opportunities. Above all, if the meeting doesn't result in real commitment to action, we must ask whether we have left any other conversation unfinished.

Improving the quality of the conversation

Conversation is a verbal dance. The word, from Latin, means 'to keep turning with'. Like any dance, it has rules and standard moves. These allow people to dance more comfortably, without stepping on each others' toes. Some rules are implicitly understood; others, particularly in group conversations, must be spelled out in detail and rehearsed. Conversation is dynamic and each participant is both speaker and listener *throughout the conversation*.

The quality of any conversation depends on the quality of the listening. The listener controls the speaker's behaviour by their own: by maintaining or breaking eye contact, by their body position, by nodding or shaking their head, by taking notes or doodling, and so on. And, when we speak, we demonstrate the quality of our listening. Look out for the signs of poor listening, in yourself as well as others. They include:

- Outright condemnation of an idea
- Replying only to a part of what somebody has said
- Interrupting
- Holding another conversation at the same time
- Evading the issue

- Using emotional words
- Falling asleep.

Any conversation consists, for each participant, of *two* parts: the external, spoken, conversation and the internal conversation in our heads. As Chair, your internal conversation will be particularly strong. As we participate in the external conversation, we may be using our internal conversation to:

- Suggest answers to problems
- Judge what the speaker is saying
- Concentrate on a part of what the speaker is saying
- Compare ideas to others we already have
- Plan the next move in the conversation
- Ask what is happening in the group.

At times, we should *stop* holding our inner conversation and listen – truly listen – to what the speaker is saying. At others, we can manage the internal conversation by taking notes of our thoughts so that we can put them to one side, vocalising our thoughts or pausing before we speak, to allow the internal conversation to happen.

The ten commandments of effective listening

1. *Stop talking*: To others; and to yourself! You cannot listen if you are talking.

2. *Demonstrate your interest*: Maintain eye contact – and expect the speaker not to. Lean forward; nod to indicate understanding. Ask questions. Take notes. But no doodling, shuffling, fiddling or looking about.

3. *Don't interrupt*: Allow pauses to happen. Try not to finish sentences for the speaker. Stop others interrupting.

4. *Put yourself in the speaker's shoes*: Imagine yourself in their position, doing their work, facing their difficulties. Imagine how they might regard you or the rest of the group.

5. *Listen to your intuition*: About the speaker's body language, tone of voice, eye contact. Test your intuition with questions, prefaced perhaps with an honest disclaimer: 'My intuition is telling me . . .'; 'I have no real evidence for this, but . . .' Be careful.

6 *Listen for 'creative triggers'*: Note down ideas that you would like to explore further. Listen for metaphors, analogies, figures of speech, evocative or emotive words that might prove interesting starting points for new conversations.

7. *Encourage*: Show you are keen for the speaker to continue. Avoid disagreeing, criticising or judging.

8. *Check your understanding*: Repeat what the speaker has just said at an appropriate point. Try to rephrase but use the speaker's language.

9. *Ask 'What's good about it?'*: Which points can you add to, build on, develop? Cultivate 'yes and' rather than 'yes but'.

10. *Stop talking*: This is first and last: all the other commandments depend on it.

Three techniques, in particular, will help you to listen better: questions, statements and summaries. Meetings often don't include enough questions. Many organisational cultures value assertiveness and decisiveness over uncertainty and doubt: to ask a question can be seen as evidence of ignorance or weakness. Yet questions are probably the most powerful tools we have to improve our thinking. They allow us to:

- Explore others' thinking
- Invite others to explore our thinking
- Make our thinking more visible to others.

We can also use them to maintain control of the conversational process by:

- Changing course
- Bringing the conversation to a halt
- Kick-starting a conversation that has got stuck
- Concentrating on a particular point
- Expanding the conversation to include a broader perspective
- Stopping people from rambling
- Inviting quieter group members to contribute.

Using questions, and encouraging others to do the same, will help to restore the balance between talking and listening.

Types of question

CLOSED
Can you . . .?/Will you . . .?
Is it . . .?/Do you . . .?
(Can only be answered 'yes' or 'no')

To obtain a 'yes' or 'no'
To establish matters of fact
To refocus the discussion
To stop rambling
To check understanding

OPEN
Why/who/what/when/where/how?
(Cannot be answered

To avoid 'yes' or 'no'
To open or widen the discussion
To encourage a contribution

'yes' or 'no')	To gain information in a non-directive way To get ideas as well as facts
SPECIFIC *At what point . . .?* *Where exactly . . .?*	Directs the discussion Prevents rambling Engages expertise Helps to bring someone into the discussion To speed up and focus attention To help a flagging moment
OVERHEAD *What do we think about . . .*	Addresses the whole group Helps to avoid embarrassment Stimulates responses from new speakers Helps make a point without sacrificing impartiality
RELAY *Thanks Gill. John, what do you think about this?*	From one speaker to another Comparing ideas Keeps the conversation moving
REVERSE *Well: what do you think?* *You think/feel . . .*	Reflects a question back to the speaker Encourages a speaker to expand or qualify

Statements are useful to define the purpose, objectives and scope of the conversation. Make any opening statement positive. Statements during items of a meeting can be used to introduce it, to give information, to temper conflict or confusion with fact, to gauge the mood of the group, to provoke, energise or stimulate discussion.

Summaries are useful for drawing the group's thinking together: to reflect on what the meeting has accomplished so far, to mark the progress of the conversation, and to signal the stages in the thinking process.

Summarising within items

Control people's contributions by summarising them, particularly when they ramble, repeat themselves or become anecdotal. Summarise to bring one part of the conversation to a close or renew its energy if it goes slack.

Summarising at the end of items

This will seal an agreement and clarify actions to be taken. This summary can usefully be made by the minute-taker: it will give them the opportunity to speak in the meeting, enhance their role and allow them to check the accuracy of their notes.

Summarising at the end of the meeting

A brief summary will bring the meeting to a positive close, reminding participants of what they have achieved and pointing the way forward to future actions.

Difficult situations

The meeting that goes exactly according to plan probably doesn't exist. These are perhaps the most serious and most common difficulties you will face.

Loss of direction

Perhaps you're having too much fun! When people start to chat, you must bring them to order. Restate the task; summarise the main ideas so far; ask direct questions. Invoke the clock.

Conflict

Adversarial thinking can easily turn into conflict. Many meetings seem to collapse into ritual recrimination almost as a matter of course. You are *not* powerless in the face of emotional hostility; but, to handle it well, you must distance yourself from it. Try to locate the source of the problem. Sometimes this is obvious: insecurity at a time of great change, stress, a new set of working relationships or pressure from public exposure. Hostility is often a sign of powerlessness. This is why anger often centres on what 'they' have done: senior management, other teams, department heads, 'rogue operators' who have bucked the system, engineers or sales staff who are never in the office . . .

Be prepared. Give yourself a single overriding objective: to empower the group to do something practical. Only by focusing their thoughts on what they *can* do will you transform people's energy into purposeful activity. Arm yourself with a few guiding principles:

- Make the objective of the meeting clear at the outset. Challenge people to explain the relevance of their remarks to the meeting's objectives

- Remember that your task is to control the conversation. Resist being drawn into the emotional maelstrom, however hard that may be

- Slow the conversation down. Don't mirror the tone, pitch or speed of others' speech. Don't interrupt or cut people off in mid-sentence

- Summarise people's points. Turn problems into 'How to' statements and focus on actions

- Stop people talking about others who are not at the meeting. Reiterate that 'they' aren't here and we are, and that only we can address our objectives.

Hidden agendas

We all go to meetings with private agendas. They are only harmful when they come into conflict with the meeting's public agenda. Good private agendas might include:

- Seeing the meeting as a career investment
- Helping the Chair achieve a successful meeting
- Strengthening the group
- Encouraging other participants.

Bad private agendas will include:

- Wanting to please
- Empire building
- Venting frustration
- Discrediting a rival
- Undermining the Chair
- Scoring points off others
- Riding a favourite hobbyhorse
- Demonstrating how overworked you are ('Poor me' . . .).

Evidence for harmful hidden agendas might include stonewalling ('I've no choice', delay, promises unfulfilled, outright refusal to act), attack (on every idea and everybody: insults, bullying, lots of bluster), and trickery (denying having said something, twisting an argument, double meanings). If you can locate the fear that causes it, you may be able to remove the agenda by removing the fear. If you can't track suspicious tactics back to their source, you may be able to show that you recognise the tactic. This may at least stop the behaviour recurring.

Hijacking

A severe loss of direction, which occurs when a private agenda attempts to take over. It may even involve a conspiracy. Everybody has a duty to rescue the meeting from hijacking. Refer to the agenda and ask for the relevance of a suspicious remark. Appeals to group solidarity should solve the problem, at least temporarily. An attempted hijack usually means that a major issue needs to be addressed. Try to identify it and decide how to tackle it. Senior management at meetings chaired by subordinates are particularly prone to hijack. The Chair *must* try to exercise proper authority. If you conduct the meeting fairly, you will have nothing to fear from a responsible senior manager – who may be assessing your leadership potential.

Groupthink

Groupthink is the drive for consensus at any cost. At times of stress – or great success – a group may suppress any ideas that threaten its own identity. People start to self-censor thoughts that they feel might be seen as 'deviant'. Consequently, the meeting's thinking becomes dangerously blinkered. Symptoms of groupthink include:

- The illusion of invulnerability

- Collective rationalisation to discount warnings

- Self-appointed Thoughtguards to suppress dissent on sight

- Pressure on 'deviance' from the norm: overt or covert

- Self-censorship of ideas or behaviour by group members

- A sense of unanimity: silence is interpreted as consent

- Self-righteousness: taking the moral high ground.

To counteract groupthink:

- Challenge the need for collective decision-making: appoint 'decision owners'

- Encourage diverse opinions systematically

- Pursue disagreements in an orderly way

- Invite outsiders or new group members to 'kick-start' change

- Ensure that the task leader or process director is willing to have their own judgements examined critically

- After the meeting, examine the procedures of the group: how often you meet; how long since you changed personnel; whether you act democratically.

Closing the meeting

Closing the meeting well is as important as opening it well. People must know exactly what will happen after the meeting, and who is responsible for making it happen. Delegate as many actions as possible. Ensure that nobody (including you!) takes on an unrealistic amount of work. Allocating responsibility to others helps to give people ownership of the work, develop individuals' skills and build the team.

Spell out precisely what actions you have agreed. If an action point remains vague, people will be uncertain what to do or wriggle out of doing it. Every action point should have an Actioner – preferably one person with responsibility for carrying it out – and a deadline – as soon as possible after the meeting.

If the conditions of satisfaction for an agreed action are unclear, you won't be able to judge whether it has happened. They should be SMART:

- Specific
- Measurable
- Agreed with the Actioner
- Realistic
- Time-related.

Finally, give the Actioner the confidence to do the task. Make it plain that you will give any support, training or explanations necessary, be available for consultation and advice and make the delegation of the task public.

Back up all decisions and actions in writing. A summary action sheet distributed with – or before – the full minutes can be useful. Others affected by the action may need to be contacted by memo or e-mail.

Now you can close the meeting. Make your final remarks positive, forward-looking – and brief!

- Summarise what has been decided and point the way ahead
- Check that the minute-taker is happy with their record of the meeting
- Set the time and date of the next meeting if necessary

  Emphasise the achievements of the meeting
- Thank everybody for attending and contributing.

Why not . . .?

  Write down every point you want to make at the start of the meeting

  Start exactly on time
- Resolve to use one technique to counter adversarial thinking

- Set up a 'yes but' box: any negative comment to cost £1. You will notice a radical improvement in the quality of the group's listening – and thinking
- Take into the meeting a list of question types – and specific questions you want to ask
- Ask Actioners to summarise back to you the actions for which they are taking responsibility, with targets and deadlines
- Make notes of your inner conversation, as a way of managing it.